GRAND CANYON
NATIONAL PARK

BONECHI

DISTRIBUTED BY:
SMITH-SOUTHWESTERN, INC.
1850 NORTH ROSEMONT
MESA, AZ 85205
800-783-3909
WWW.SMITH-SOUTHWESTERN.COM

ISBN 1-56274-781-9

Project and editorial conception: *Casa Editrice Bonechi*
Publication Manager: *Monica Bonechi*
Picture research: *Monica Bonechi*
Graphic design, make-up and cover: *Sonia Gottardo*
Editing: *Patrizia Fabbri*
Drawings and map by: *Studio Grafico Daniela Mariani - Pistoia*
Text by: *Hugh Crandall*

© Copyright by Casa Editrice Bonechi - Florence - Italy
E-mail: bonechi@bonechi.it

Printed in Italy by *Centro Stampa Editoriale Bonechi.*

Photographs from the archives of *Casa Editrice Bonechi* taken
by *Andrea Pistolesi.*
Photographs on pages 1, 15 bottom, 54-55, 56-57:
Andrea Innocenti.
Photographs on pages 6, 7, 9: *Grand Canyon National Park.*
Photographs on pages 4-5, 10-11, 14, 15 top, 16, 29, 30-31,
40-41, 60-61: *Mike Buchheit.*

The publisher apologizes for any omissions and is willing to
make amends with the formal recognition of the author
of any photo subsequently identified.

Internet: www.bonechi.com

A 10 9 8 7 6 5 4 3 2 1

Introduction

Some things need to be seen to be believed, but even in plain sight the Grand Canyon of the Colorado River seems unbelievable. It's too vast for easy comprehension. And full understanding is made even more difficult because anything on that large a scale is too complex to be just one thing.

The Grand Canyon is the North Rim and the South Rim and the Inner Gorge and the River.

It is a tassel-eared squirrel and a big horn sheep and a chuckwalla lizard. It is a spectrum of life zones ranging from boreal forest to tropical desert. It is a textbook of geology, a museum of archeology, a laboratory of paleontology.

It is probably the world's most impressive example of the erosive power of water. And far down there, 1 mile (1.6 kilometers) below the rim, that narrow thread is the instrument of its creation. Because the Grand Canyon, after all, is a river valley. For perhaps five million years the Colorado has been cutting ever deeper into the slowly rising land, and the runoff of rains and melting snows has been crumbling the walls. During that five million years of grinding and polishing, the river has exposed a record of the last two billion years of activity in this part of the earth. During only a minuscule bit of that time has the Canyon known the presence of humans. 4,000 years ago indigenous Americans left figurines made of bound willow twigs in a cave within the gorge. It is presumed that human activity in the area has continued with only infrequent interruption from that date to the present.

The earliest record of European people at Grand Canyon is a 1540-visit by a Spanish explorer, Garcia Lopez de Cardenas, but serious exploration of the region did not begin until near the middle of the 19th century. Human presence gradually increased over the years. Sporadic exploration efforts prompted equally sporadic exploitation projects until a growing movement toward preservation culminated in the establishment of Grand Canyon National Park in 1919. Today, four million visitors a year experience the awe-inspiring splendor of this incredible product of the earth's inventive artistry.

the Grand Canyon

The history of the Grand Canyon properly begins with its pre-history, the archeological records of the indigenous peoples of the North American continent. In 1933 some figurines formed of split willow twigs were discovered in a limestone cave within the gorge. Carbon dating later established their age at about 4,000 years. The next positive evidence of mankind in the Canyon shows that a group of Anasazi or Pueblos arrived in the area some 2,500 years later. During the years between there must surely have been at least scattered occupation of the Canyon, but no proof has yet been found.

The newcomers probably drifted in from the desert lying to the southeast. They were much more culturally advanced than the earlier peoples. They made baskets and fired pots; they had developed the bow and arrow; although they were still largely hunters and gatherers, they also raised crops. A little later the Anasazi were joined by a group from the south, the Cohonina, who were only slightly less advanced and were quick to adopt the more efficient ways of their neighbors. Then, about 1150 AD, for some reason that is still a mystery, all settlements in and near the canyon were abandoned. For more than 150 years the region was uninhabited. Perhaps it was a series of dry years that drove people to more hospitable land, because the Anasazi are known to have established themselves along more reliable waterways farther to the east. About that time the Cohonina disappeared from the archeological record.

Near 1300 AD the Cerbat people moved up from the deserts along the Lower Colorado to the high plateaus formerly occupied by the Anasazi and the Cohonina – and by the split-willow people before them. They called themselves the Pai and their descendants are the Hualapai and the Havasupai who now live beside and within the Grand Canyon.

While the Cerbat were colonizing the southern rim of the Canyon, Paiute from well north of the Canyon spread south to the northern rim and established a way of life much like their neighbors south of the river. From artefacts found in sites on both sides of the Colorado it has been learned that there was communication and trade across the river between the Cerbat and the Paiute and between both groups and the Anasazi and the Hopi to the east.

Recorded history of the Grand Canyon begins with the chronicles of Castaneda, the official scribe of the expedition of the Spanish explorer, Francisco Coronado. At the head of a great entourage of soldiers and Native Americans he had ridden north from the lands of the Aztecs and, in the summer of 1540, he reached the pueblo of Zuni in what is now New Mexico. There he heard about the Hopi people to the west and sent one of his lieutenants, Pedro de Tovar, to investigate. Tovar, the first European to visit the Hopi, learned of a great river to the west. Coronado then sent another lieutenant, Garcia Lopez de Cardenas, to investigate. With Hopi to guide him, Cardenas travelled west for 20 days before becoming the first European to see the Canyon, probably in the vicinity of Desert View. He spent three days trying to reach the river far below, but got only a third of the way down. He reported that the gorge was three to four leagues (7.5 to 10 miles, 12 to 16 kilometers) wide. But, since Coronado was in search of gold to replenish Spain's dwindling treasury, the expedition pressed on without further investigation. Over 200 years later Father Francisco Garces made a trip from southern Arizona to the California missions and, intending to return by way of Zuni, spent several days among the Walapai and the Havasupai in their Grand Canyon homes.

That same year, 1776, two other Franciscan priests, Silvestre Velez de Escalante and Francisco Atanasio Dominguez, rode north from Santa Fe in search of an easy route to northern California. Near Great Salt Lake they gave up and headed home by first going directly south. Among the Paiute of northern Arizona they learned of the impassibility of the great canyon ahead and turned east without seeing it. They crossed the Colorado at a ford now under the waters of Lake Powell and returned to Santa Fe by way of the Hopi villages.

Another 50 years would pass before American trappers would be in the Grand Canyon area – Kit Carson, Jedediah Smith, Antoine Leroux, Bill Williams, James Ohio Pattie – but their reports were meager, mostly verbal, and often exaggerated. Even after Mexico ceded the area to the United States in 1848, several official exploratory expeditions only passed close to the Canyon without actually seeing it.

Then, in 1857-1858, a government expedition under Lieutenant Joseph Ives tested the navigability of the Colorado in a small steamboat, Explorer. 350 miles upriver the boat struck a rock and had to be abandoned. Ives and his men continued eastward on foot. His party included a German artist, von Egglofstein, and a geologist, Dr. John Newberry, the first scientist to study the "Big Canyon" as Ives named it. They visited among the Havasupai and, with the help of Hualapai guides, members of the group reached the bottom of the Canyon at Diamond Creek.

Two other significant explorations of the Grand Canyon were also made by way of the Colorado River, but they

Two men at Tuweep.

Two of Powell's boats on the beach.

First passenger train (17 September, 1901).

started down the river from farther north. In 1869 and again in 1871 Major John Wesley Powell conducted flotillas of small, wooden boats down the Green and Colorado Rivers to map the area and investigate its geology and ecology.

Increasing excursions into their territory made the Hualapai and the Havasupai nervous, and from 1866 until they were defeated in 1869, they warred with the US Army. Reservations were established for both tribes in 1882.

During that time, when the Native Americans were being forcibly relieved of their stewardship of the Grand Canyon, the European Americans were also beginning to compete with each other for control. In 1882, 1883, and 1886, Senator Benjamin Harrison of Indiana introduced bills in Congress to make the Canyon a national park. But in 1883, John Hance started mining asbestos at the bottom of the canyon and William Bass registered claims for asbestos and

copper on both sides of the river. Soon Hance and Bass were also providing guide services for visitors. Many other mining claims were recorded and the Canyon began to assume economic potential. Because of the political effect of such commercial interests, Senator Harrison's bills failed to pass.

A topographic survey party in the early 1870's and a US Geological Survey in 1880 completed the mapping begun by Major Powell. Thomas Moran, the young artist whose work had helped alert the American public to the magnificence of Yellowstone, was a member of both expeditions and his paintings again helped arouse public interest in an outstanding element of the American landscape.

Clarence E. Dutton, the highly respected geologist who had conducted the second expedition, was the first to see in the enormous stone formations that had been left by the erosion of the layers of rock a resemblance to the temple architecture of India and China and, therefore, to religious symbolism in general. We have him to thank for names like Vishnu Temple, Brahma Temple, Wotan's Throne, Tower of Babel, and Tower of Ra.

Eventually, mining operations proved to be unprofitable and the former miners turned to tourism. Two hotels were built along the rim and passenger stage service from Flagstaff was begun. In 1901 the Santa Fe Railroad completed a spur track from Williams to a point on the rim between Yaki Point and Yavapai Point. By 1905 the El Tovar Hotel was completed, as were also Hopi House, Babbitt's store, Kolb Brothers photographic studio, and Vercamp's curio store. Grand Canyon Village was established.

The North Rim developed somewhat differently. A number of livestock companies brought cattle and sheep onto the grasslands of the Kaibab and Kanab plateaus and operated profitably until the range was destroyed by overgrazing. Some estimates indicated that, in the 1890's, over 100,000 head of cattle and over 250,000 sheep were grazing what is essentially fragile land. By 1906 most ranching had stopped because the formerly lush grassland had become desolate stretches of sagebrush. Stimulated by increasing reports of both the uniqueness of the region and its vulnerability, the movement toward official preservation gained impetus.

When Senator Harrison became president in 1893, he established by proclamation the Grand Canyon Forest Preserve. President Theodore Roosevelt, after a visit to the Canyon in 1903, expanded protection by proclaiming the Forest Preserve first a Game Preserve in 1906 and then a National Monument in 1908. Congress finally designated it a National Park in February of 1919.

A new Grand Canyon National Monument was established west of the park in 1932 and Marble Canyon National Monument was created in 1969. Legislation in 1975 increased the size of the park by adding to it those two monuments and portions of other public lands. The same legislation took 84,000 acres (34,000 hectares) from the park to expand the Havasupai reservation. The present size of the park is about 1,218,000 acres (493,000 hectares).

Since the Grand Canyon has been under the protective management of the National Park Service, human-caused changes in its appearance and facilities have been primarily those necessary to accommodate the yearly influx of more than four million visitors from all over the world. Since nature-caused changes take place very slowly, the Canyon itself is still the grand and mysterious wonder people have known for at least 4,000 years.

JOHN WESLEY POWELL

Some of the exploration of Grand Canyon has always been done by way of the river itself. Despite the dangers of impossible rapids and raging floods, in the late 19th and early 20th centuries it still seemed the easiest way to study the great gorge. After the Civil War much of the attention of the nation was directed toward the sparsely populated, often still unknown, western lands. One blank space on the maps was the vast drainage system comprising the Colorado River and its principal tributaries, the Green and the Grand.

Major John Wesley Powell, a 34-year-old school teacher who, despite having lost his right hand and forearm during the war, remained an intrepid amateur explorer and river runner, and was fascinated with the idea of filling in that blank space. He was also, because of a vocational interest, remarkably well educated in geology, biology, and paleontology. He was, in short, perhaps the most qualified man at that time to lead a river exploration of unknown lands. He spent his own money having special boats built and, through his wartime acquaintanceship with General U. S. Grant, arranged to have supplies available at a few points along his intended route. With a diverse crew of nine men, Powell set forth in four boats on May 24, 1869, from Green River, Wyoming. His plan was to follow the Green River down to its confluence with what was then called the Grand River, but is now considered the upper extension of the Colorado, and then to follow the river through

its fabled Grand Canyon to the rolling hills west of the Colorado Plateau. It was an arduous journey. Within two weeks they had lost one boat with all its equipment and supplies and almost lost its three passengers. That episode was followed by a month of seemingly endless rapids, some of which they ran but many of which had to be portaged. Then, at the mouth of the Uinta River, they were able to rest for three days and obtain a few additional supplies. One man abandoned the project at this time. During the next six weeks of hardship three men were given permission to leave the expedition and one of the three remaining boats was abandoned. Throughout the trip they were forced to fish and hunt game in order to keep themselves adequately fed. But during all that time Powell and his crew carefully mapped the course of the rivers, measured the heights of river banks and the thicknesses of rock strata, and took copious notes describing the fossils they found and the living plants and animals they encountered.

When the remaining six exhausted men in their two battered boats pulled ashore at the mouth of the Virgin River on August 29, 1869, one large space on the map was blank no longer. John Wesley Powell obtained government support for a second Colorado River expedition in 1871-1872 and chronicled both trips in a best-selling book. He helped organize the US Geological Survey and was appointed its second director. During the same period he created the Bureau of American Ethnography within the Smithsonian Institute and was appointed its first director. He retired because of ill health in 1894 and died quietly at his summer home in Maine in 1902.

the rocky giants

Geologists and people who begin to think of geological events have to make an adjustment in their concept of time. The earth is not at all static, but except for catastrophic events like earthquakes and volcanic eruptions, it moves in action and reaction with truly unimaginable slowness. At any given place on earth, most of that movement seems to be simple rising above and sinking below sea level. Occasionally mountains are built in one or another of several ways. When the surface is under water, it collects sediments; when it is above water, it is worn down by erosion. And that brings us to the Grand Canyon. The land that includes the Kaibab Plateau of the North Rim and the Coconino Plateau of the South Rim has been sinking and rising for many millions of years. It last began to rise some 200 million years ago. For the most recent six million of those years this busy river has been using the sand and mud and rocks of the high country to the north to carve a groove through the rising land. It then has carried its grinding tools away to become sediments in a different sea, just now known as the Gulf of California. As it has carved deeper and deeper it has revealed older and older layers of rocks that were formed by compaction and cementing of sediments that were deposited in older seas. Major Powell spoke of the layered rock of the Grand Canyon as "the pages of a great stone book." If so, it is a book that is remarkably well preserved, considering its great age, although the forces of earth have used it harshly from time to time and a few of its pages are missing. Also it is a book that most of us can not read; it must be read to us the way fairy tales were read to us by our parents. To continue the analogy for a moment, this is the story the scientists have read to us from those stony pages. Once upon a time a long, long time ago, 2,000 million years ago in fact, the surface of the earth in this area was a more or less flat layer of

intrusions became Zoroaster Gneiss. Over the next 500 million years the mountains were worn down and the land again became a nearly level plain near sea level. That plain was then submerged beneath a sea for long enough to accumulate sediments that became at least 28 miles (4,500 meters) of rock. These rocks are now known as the Grand Canyon Supergroup. At this point in our story another mountain building period began, but this time the earth used a different method. Instead of compressing the crust until it

volcanic and sedimentary rock. During the next 300 million years it was heaved and distorted by compression into high mountains. The once horizontal layers of sediment were warped nearly vertical in places and their rocks were changed by heat and pressure. Molten rock was forced upward through cracks and that, too, was changed. The layered material became the metamorphic rock today called Vishnu Schist and the

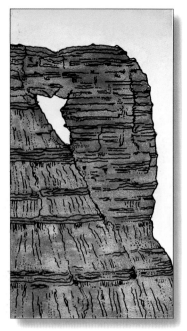

folded upward like a rug pushed from both sides, it stretched the crust until it cracked into blocks. The blocks then tilted some 12 or 15 degrees, one edge rising while the other sank, to form a series of fault block mountains. They, of course, began immediately to be worn back to the flat surface that a quiet earth seems to prefer. We have now covered some 800 million years of events and the wearing down will take another 400 million.

That will bring us to the beginning of the Cambrian age of the Paleozoic Era and we find our bit of the Earth again under water. For the next 700 to 800 million years the principal activity of this section of the earth's crust will be a settling of the land below sea level and a rising and a settling again and a rising. Each time the land was under water is recorded in the strata of rocks made from the sediments collected on the sea floor. And also in those rocks is recorded a great deal of information about the life that swam in those ancient seas and the life that walked or crawled on the mud flats or sand dunes at the sea's edge. Geologists can read in those strata the rate at which the shoreline moved eastward as the land sank. Sandstones develop from deposits laid down close to shore in a shallow sea, shales from the mud carried farther out, and limestones from deposits far out in deep water. It is also known that 40 inches (a meter) of sandstone accumulates about every 1,500 years, 40 inches (a meter) of shale every 3,000 years, and 40 inches (a meter) of limestone every 7,500 years. Just above the tilted strata of the Grand Canyon Supergroup (the rocks that were lifted into fault block mountains and then worn away to nearly level) is 98 to 295 feet (30 to 90 meters) of Tapeats Sandstone laid down in the coastal shallows of the sea that advanced from the west. Above that is 197 to 460 feet (60 to 140 meters) of Bright Angel Shale, deposited as the land continued to sink and the coast line moved farther east. Next, reading upward, are several strata of limestone as the land sank to its maximum depth and began to rise. There is Muav Limestone, up to 820 feet (250 meters) thick; Temple Butte Limestone, 98 to 984 feet (30 to 300 meters) thick; and Redwall Limestone, 394 to 656 feet (120 to 200 meters) thick. By this time, about 330 million years ago, the rising land had made the sea shallow again and a mixed group of red sandstone and red siltstone called the Supai group was laid down. Above that is a layer of bright red siltstone called Hermit Shale. It is the red that leached out of these layers and washed down across the gray limestone below it that has caused the limestone to be called "Redwall". Some 270 million years ago the land rose above water for a while and the next layer is Coconino Sandstone that preserves the record of a large desert that once lay in great dunes across what is now northern Arizona. The tracks of many small reptiles have been fossilized in this formation. Then the sea again moved in from the west and 260 million years ago laid down a 197-foot (60-meter) deep mix of sandstones and limestones called the Toroweap Formation.

Above that is almost 328 feet (100 meters) of Kaibab Limestone, deposited between 250 and 100 million years ago. At the beginning of the Cenozoic Era, about 70 million years ago, the long quiet period ended with the Laramide Orogeny, the 20 million years of mountain building in which the Rocky Mountains were formed. During that time a huge portion of the earth's crust was squeezed from east and west and buckled upward into the Colorado Plateau. The ancestral Colorado River once flowed along the eastern edge of the plateau to drain into a land-locked basin that has been named Lake Bidahochi. The west side of the plateau drained toward the Pacific Ocean. About 25 million years ago the land west of the plateau, now known as the Basin and Range Province, was subjected to tension that broke it into blocks. At that time the Colorado Plateau was both cracked into faults and raised a little higher, leaving the western edge considerably lower than the bed of the Colorado on the east. The Hualapai drainage system on the west side of the Plateau gradually extended farther and farther east through headwater erosion, until it linked with streams draining the eastern side. What then occurred is known as "stream capture". Because the land west of the Plateau was lower than the land to the east, the eastern streams reversed their direction and the Colorado began to flow westward toward the Gulf of California. It was "captured" by the Hualapai drainage system. The lower part of the ancestral Colorado became what is now the Little Colorado and also reversed direction of flow to begin to drain Lake Bidahochi. It is believed the linkage of the eastern and western drainage systems of the Colorado Plateau was completed about six million years ago and the carving of the Grand Canyon began in earnest. The Colorado River system drains a total area of about 237,000 square miles (615,000 square kilometers). The river is 1,448 miles (2,330 kilometers) long, of which 280 miles (450 kilometers) are in the Grand Canyon where it slices through the southern end of the Colorado Plateau.

THICKNESS (feet)	DEPOSITIONAL ENVIRONMENT	AGE (million of years ago)	GEOLOGIC TIME Era	GEOLOGIC TIME Period
300-500	sea	250	PALEOZOIC	Middle Permian
250-450	sea	260		Middle Permian
50-350	desert	270		Early Permian
250-1,000	floodplain	280		Early Permian
950-1,350	swamp	300		Early Permian
				Pennsylvanian
450-700	sea	330		Early and middle Mississippian
30-1,000	sea	370		Late Devonian
DISCONFORMITY		400-500		Silurian and Orodovician
50-1,000	sea	530		Middle Cambrian
200-450	sea	540		Early and Middle Cambrian
100-300	sea	550		Early Cambrian
THE GREAT UNCONFORMITY		570-800		
15,000	sea	800-1,200	PRECAMBRIAN	Late
	metamorphosed sea sediments	1,700		Early
	molten intrusion			

North Rim — South Rim — Grand Canyon — Colorado River

KAIBAB LIMESTONE
TOROWEAP FORMATION
COCONINO SANDSTONE
HERMIT SHALE
SUPAI GROUP
REDWALL LIMESTONE
TEMPLE BUTTE LIMESTONE
MUAV LIMESTONE
BRIGHT ANGEL SHALE
TAPEATS SANDSTONE
GRAND CANYON SUPERGROUP
VISHNU SCHIST
ZOROASTER GRANITE

Untamed nature

*B*ecause elevations within the Grand Canyon vary from
8,860 feet (2,700 meters) on the North Rim to only
1,210 feet (370 meters) at the river's edge, the biotic
communities vary from boreal forest to hot, arid desert. A
rule of thumb has it that a 984-foot (300-meter) change in
elevation is equal to a move of 300 miles (480 kilometers)
north or south. So the flora of the Canyon is like that of
northern Canada on parts of the North Rim and like that of
the desert of Mexico in the bottom of the gorge. An additional
biotic diversity is the result of variation in precipitation. The
North Rim gets about 26 inches (67 cm) per year, most of it
as snow, while deep in the chasm less than (10 inches) 25 cm
per year falls in infrequent rains. But, even in the driest areas,
streams, springs, and seepages create moist micro-habitats
in which water-loving plants can thrive. So, depending on
where you are in the Grand Canyon, you can expect to see
spruce trees and aspen or ponderosa pine or pinyon pine
and juniper or sagebrush and cactus – or even cottonwood
and willows. But those are only the obvious, dominant flora.
At least 1,500 different kinds of plants have been identified
within the Canyon and along the rims. Blue lupine and red
paintbrush and purple asters grow among ferns in the
forest clearings. Down along the river many plants common
to areas farther north have had their seeds brought in by
the river or by migratory birds and have found a home. So
Great Basin sagebrush and shadscale grow side by side with
creosote bush, ocotillo, and prickly pear. And just a few feet
away where a spring runoff joins the river, columbine and
maidenhair fern grow beside poison ivy under a redbud tree.
An area with as diverse a selection of plants as the Grand
Canyon can be expected to have an equally varied population
of animals. It is, therefore, not surprising that the national
park at last count is home for 17 fishes, 6 amphibians, 35
reptiles, 76 mammals, and 284 birds (including migrants).
Among the birds can be found tiny hummingbirds feeding on
thistle blossoms, both bald and golden eagles, the once rare
peregrine falcon, and wild turkeys feeding on the forest floor.
The tassel-eared squirrel is unique to the Grand Canyon. It
comes in two varieties, the Abert Squirrel on the South Rim
and the Kaibab Squirrel on the North Rim. They are members
of the ponderosa pine ecosystem, feeding principally on
pine nuts. The Grand Canyon rattlesnake is also unique. Its
unusual salmon color is thought to be an adaptation to the
many red and pink rocks among which it lives. Mule deer are
common. In years past, because of a misguided program of
predator extermination, deer greatly overpopulated the area.
They did severe damage to the range and, during one ten-
year period, some 90,000 died of starvation. Land managers
today have a better grasp of ecosystem interrelationships and
have allowed the predators to return and the community is in
better balance. Among the predators once nearly eliminated
but now returned are mountain lions, bobcats, coyotes, and
eagles. Only the wolf is still missing from the ecosystem.
But under the conservationist management of the National
Park Service the animals of the Canyon will continue to
occupy their historic niches within the many ecological
communities the Grand Canyon provides.

in the Grand Canyon

Grand Canyon excursions

The Grand Canyon, with its rocks shaped by thousands of years of rains and floods, represents one of the most spectacular natural environments in the United States, and perhaps in the entire world, while its ardous tracks winding up to the top of the toughest heights hold a special fascination for the most experienced hikers. Equipped with adequate gear for trekking, and not forgetting an abundant supply of water, climbing in the Grand Canyon is a demanding experience requiring good training and considerable physical effort but, with the reward of magnificent breath-taking views, is quite unique. Another famous attraction of the Canyon, the exciting river route for rafts which cross it by water, also provides the visitor with truly memorable emotions. Starting from Whitmore Canyon, special crafts capable of carrying up to 18 people, ride the currents right up to Pierce Ferry on Lake Mead. For those who love nature, this is the ideal way to see the quite unique and spectacular scenery of the Grand Canyon.

THE SOUTH RIM

Whether travelling by stagecoach, by train, or by automobile, most of the many millions of visitors to the Grand Canyon have arrived first at the South Rim. From its edge they have gazed in awe far down into the great chasm at the faint ribbon of water winding among its many bizarre creations. Because the Colorado Plateau slopes toward the south, the South Rim is 985-1,312 feet (300-400 meters) lower than the North Rim and provides a fine view of the ragged, deeply eroded northern slope of the Canyon.

It is a view to stimulate wonder and humility, and it is anticipation of this view that brings people to stand in amazed appreciation on the Canyon's Rim.

The approach from Williams or Flagstaff along wide level roads through the Kaibab National Forest with its miles of ponderosa pine trees gives no indication of what lies ahead. Suddenly the vast chasm is just there at your feet and stretching in splendor to the horizon. Since the Coconino Plateau side of the Colorado is drained down-slope toward the south, there are few streams to enter the river from the south and, therefore, less bank erosion than has occurred on the Kaibab Plateau side. The South Rim also gets less precipitation (about 14 ½ inches, 37 cm) than the North Rim (about 27 inches, 68 cm) and less than half as much snow to melt and run off in springtime floods. So the South Rim is steeper and closer to the river than the North Rim. Nearly 1 mile (1.5 km) below the South Rim, the river averages only 2 ½ miles (4 km) north of the Rim. That 21-degree slope seems much steeper. From the beginning, the Grand Canyon has been fascinating enough to be observed longer than just briefly and from only one place. So, over the years, facilities have developed to permit both longer and deeper investigation into the nature of the Canyon. There are hotel accommodations, museums, a drive along the rim, a trail down to the river, even an airport from which to make a helicopter ride over the Canyon. The National Park Service mission is in two parts which, unfortunately, are mutually incompatible. It is directed to make the area available for the enjoyment of people – and it is also directed to preserve the land in its natural state. Every road or building that complies with the first part violates the second. So the facilities on the South Rim are a compromise. They do not meet the criteria for a luxurious destination resort. Neither do they materially degrade the appearance of the natural world nor disrupt its normal functioning.

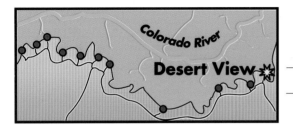

DESERT VIEW

(Elevation: 7,428 feet - 2,267 meters)

Many visitors to the Grand Canyon today drive north from Flagstaff through the Navajo Reservation and reach the South Rim at Desert View, the eastern end of the Rim Drive. It's a good place from which to begin to understand this unusual bit of our world.

To the east the land is low and nearly level in a region called the Marble Platform and the Painted Desert. Then, in a smooth, sweeping curve, it rises nearly 1,310 feet (400 meters) to become the Kaibab Plateau and again seems level. That curved rise is the East Kaibab Monocline. Some 65 million years ago the earth's crust here was squeezed from east and west with enough force to cause it to fold upward and become the high ground through which the Colorado River would later carve its way.

Seven miles east of Desert View the brown water of the untamed Little Colorado River flows north into clear, green water flowing west. The contrast in the color of the water demonstrates the effect of the Glen Canyon Dam on the river that was once so laden with red-brown silt as to be named "Colorado." Now, that heavy load of debris from the canyonlands to the north falls out of suspension and is gradually filling Lake Powell.

The watchtower on the promontory, because of its design and construction, is a reminder that this was, and still is to a large extent, the land of a people different from the European peoples who are now developing the area. Designer Mary Jane Colter conceived the tower as a "re-creation" of prehistoric American structures she had studied. The stonework, although in this case supported by a steel frame, is authentic and the interior murals are the work of the Hopi artist, Fred Kabotie.

Desert View can supply answers, but it mostly stimulates questions, and the visitor turns west along the Rim in search of assurance that what seems incredible really can be explained.

19

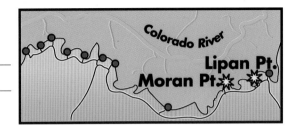

LIPAN POINT

(Elevation: 7,360 feet - 2,243 meters)

The stream that empties into the Colorado River almost directly below Lipan Point is Seventy-five Mile Creek. It is one of the many slope drainages that have no names other than their distances from Lee's Ferry, which has been arbitrarily selected as the zero milepost for travel on the river. Beyond Escalante Butte, which projects from the Canyon wall just north of Seventy-five Mile Creek, the Colorado makes an S-turn, in the middle of which is Unkar Rapids, a drop of 25 feet (7.6 meters) in a quarter mile (0.4 km). Lipan Point is the trailhead of the nine-mile Tanner Trail down to the gravelly delta at the mouth of Unkar Creek. On that delta are ruins left by the Anasazi over a thousand years ago.

A little to the right, beyond the S-turn, at the foot of the pile of horizontal strata which has been named Apollo Temple, it can be seen that the rock layers are angled downward to the right. Between those angled strata of the Pre-Cambrian Grand Canyon Supergroup and the horizontal layer of Tapeats Sandstone just above them is a gap of 500 million years that Major Powell called the Great Unconformity.

Leaving Lipan Point, by way of contrast, the snow-capped San Francisco Peaks can be seen, far to the south near Flagstaff.

MORAN POINT

(Elevation: 7,157 feet - 2,181 meters)

Thomas Moran was a 19th Century American landscape painter whose expressive work has been instrumental in persuading Americans and their representatives in Congress that some parts of their wide land merited preservation. Yellowstone, the world's first national park, owes its existence in great part to Moran's dramatic depictions of its wonders. And so does Grand Canyon National Park.

Moran said that he felt challenged by the subtle colors and the constantly changing light of the Canyon and was prompted to change his style because of its demands on the artist. This point, with its view of Red Canyon, Hance Rapids, Coronado Butte, and Sinking Ship, was one of his favorite arenas for facing that challenge.

Captain John Hance, for whom Hance Rapids and Hance Canyon are named, was the first European American to settle at Grand Canyon. He established a residence at a spring just west of Moran Point in 1883. Originally a prospector, he found tourism more profitable and guided visitors into the Canyon by way of the trails he built down to the river.

TUSAYAN RUINS

Not quite 3 ½ miles (6 km) from Moran Point is one of the last locations in the Grand Canyon area to be inhabited by the Anasazi before they relocated farther to the east on or near the present Hopi Reservation. It was excavated in 1930 by Emile W. Haury.
"Anasazi" is a Navajo word meaning "ancient ones" and the Anasazi were probably direct ancestors of present day Hopis. They moved into the Canyon about 500 AD and lived throughout the area until about 1150.
During their stay along this part of the Colorado River they became more and more dependent on the cultivation of crops, and thus on water. It is believed that a series of particularly dry years drove them east in search of a more dependable water supply, which they found among the Hopi Springs in what is now central New Mexico.
The excavated site is one of over 2,000 Anasazi constructs that have been found on both rims and within the Canyon. Some are believed to have been occupied only seasonally while crops were tended and harvested. Others were year-round dwellings and store houses.
Anasazi buildings were constructed of stones, mortared together with mud. The roofs were of large beams covered first with sticks, then bark, then mud. Their year-round structures were often L-shaped or C-shaped, open to the south and large enough to house several families and their supplies of stored food. They were fine basket weavers and potters and, after the introduction of cotton from Mexico, developed techniques of spinning and weaving.
The museum at Tusayan Ruins contains exhibits featuring not only Anasazi culture, but also demonstrating artefacts and life styles of other primitive and modern Native Americans of the Grand Canyon and the surrounding region.
Visitors may follow a self-guided trail through the ruin. Park Service Interpretive Rangers also give frequent explanatory talks.

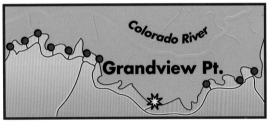

GRANDVIEW POINT

(Elevation: 7,406 feet - 2,257 meters)

Vagaries of the air currents through the Canyon seem to bring Grandview Point a bit more precipitation than most of the eastern South Rim. As a consequence, the ponderosa pine forest is thicker here, and grows nearly up to the edge. Clumps of Gambel oak are interspersed among the pines.

At the very edge it is warmer and drier so pinyon pine and juniper dominate.

In the early years this was the center of visitor activity. In 1890 Peter Berry staked a mining claim on Horseshoe Mesa just below Grandview Point. For seven years he extracted some of the nation's richest copper ore from his mine.

But operating costs in such a remote and difficult location were too high to make even the finest ore profitable, so Berry entered the tourist business. He built the two-story Grand View Hotel and for several years was the proprietor of the dominant tourist center at the Canyon.

The completion of the railroad to the South Rim in 1901 and the subsequent development of Grand Canyon Village gradually took more and more business away from Berry and he closed

both the hotel and the mine in 1908.

As the name Grandview suggests, the view of the Grand Canyon from this point is considered to be one of the finest available. The panorama extends unbroken from Desert View to the east with the Marble Platform beyond to Shoshone Point far down river to the west.

Details of the North Rim and the Canyon's many fantastic erosional formations with their fanciful names are particularly clear in morning light.

Slightly to the right of Horseshoe Mesa, which is almost directly below, is the eroded gorge of Hance Creek leading down to the Colorado. Just beyond the V of the creek valley is the far bank of the river. This point is geologically interesting because the rock that is lowest and with faintly vertical striations is Vishnu Schist, the two-billion-year-old bed rock of the area.

Directly above it is a horizontal layer of Bass Limestone, part of the Grand Canyon Supergroup of the late Pre-Cambrian period.

This is the earlier of the two prominent geologic unconformities of the region. Major Powell's Great Unconformity is of a later time.

YAKI POINT

(Elevation: 7,260 feet - 2,212 meters)

Yaki Point offers another superb view of the central section of the Grand Canyon. Across the Canyon and to the right is the large flat-topped butte which was named Wotan's Throne by Francois Matthes, a scientist and a member of the first US Geological Survey mapping expedition to the Canyon. Just to its right is another prominent butte which was named Vishnu Temple by Clarence E. Dutton, a geologist and disciple of Major Powell.

Down below Yaki Point is the relatively gentle slope of the Tonto Platform, made from the broad strata of gray-green Bright Angel Shale. The Tonto Trail,

the longest in Grand Canyon National Park, runs along this plateau for 72 miles (116 km) from Garnet Canyon at the west end to Red Canyon to the east. Sections of another trail, the South Kaibab, can also be seen from the overlook. The South Kaibab is one of the three trails that link the South and North Rims together, by way of suspension bridges across the Colorado River. The trailhead is up a side road about half a mile (0.8 km) south of Yaki Point. It was completed by the Park Service in 1925. Until that time the only safe trail from the South Rim to the bottom of the Canyon was the Cameron Toll Road, known

originally and again today as the Bright Angel Trail. The Kaibab Trail was built to a large extent to break Ralph Cameron's monopoly on easy access to the inner Canyon and the river. To the west below Yaki Point overlook is Pipe Creek, so named because of a practical joke. In the late 19th century, sometime around 1890, Pete Berry, the Cameron brothers, and Mike McClure were walking along the Tonto Trail when Ralph Cameron, ahead of the others, found a meerschaum pipe in the bed of a small, then unnamed, stream he was crossing. He quickly carved a date in the late 18th century on the pipe and left it for one of the others to find. One of them did, and the three wondered for some time who could possibly have lost his pipe there a hundred years before.

THE SOUTH RIM FOREST

The South Rim is the northern edge of the Coconino Plateau which, in turn is the southern end of the uplifted land the geologists have named the Colorado Plateau. For the most part, the semi-arid climate of the Coconino region supports a dominant vegetative cover of pinyon pine and Utah juniper and associated high desert plants.

Near the Rim, however, and for several miles south, the elevation is almost too high for the pinyon-juniper ecosystem and precipitation is sufficient to provide conditions that are marginally suitable for the ponderosa pine. Its deep, spreading root system allows the ponderosa to tolerate dryer conditions than most large, temperate-climate pines.

Right at the edge of the Canyon warm, dry updrafts cause conditions better suited to the pinyons and junipers and they reassert dominance. Scrub oaks are found within both life communities but are more apt to occur as thickets among the ponderosas. Yucca, cliffrose, Mormon tea, mountain mahogany, and big sagebrush are common in the understory of the pinyon-juniper forest.

Both ground squirrels and tree squirrels are among the small mammal populations of the South Rim forest. The Abert squirrel is the South Rim variety of the tassel-eared tree squirrel that is unique to the Grand Canyon area. Both it and the Kaibab squirrel of the North Rim are residents of the ponderosa pine ecosystem, largely relying on pine nuts for survival. During the last glacial age, when a much cooler, wetter climate allowed the ponderosas to grow all the way to the bottom of the Canyon, the tassel-eared squirrels were one contiguous population.

Then climatic changes made the lower Canyon untenable for the pine forest, creating a gap which separated the squirrels into two groups with slightly different gene pools. The groups have become enough different in appearance and habits that they may some day be classified as two distinct species.

The Abert squirrel of the South Rim has a dark head, upper body and upper tail with belly, feet, and underside of the tail almost white. It seems to have a more diverse diet than its Kaibab cousin, a few uncrossable miles away.

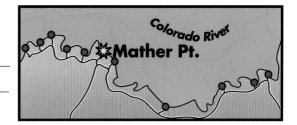

MATHER POINT

(Elevation: 7,120 feet - 2,170 meters)

Mather Point is named in honor of the first director of the National Park Service, Stephen T. Mather. Because most visitors to Grand Canyon arrive on the South Rim at Grand Canyon Village and the Mather Center, their first view of the gorge is apt to be from this spot.

Only a fourth of the Canyon can be seen from Mather Point, but that much is ample to convince them that they were right to have come to see this "Seventh Wonder of the Natural World."

After a period of just staring in wonder, many visitors find time to think of numbers – of dimensions.

Straight out there the North Rim is 10 miles (16 km) away – as that raven soaring in the updrafts at the Canyon edge would fly.

That tiny thread of water far down there is actually about 295 feet (90 meters) wide. It is almost 1 mile (1.5 km) lower than Mather Point and only 3 miles (5 km) away in a line of sight that is depressed nearly 21 degrees.

It seems much steeper.

The average depth of the river is 50 feet (15 meters) but it has been measured at 112 feet (34 meters) in one place.

The average speed of the river is 3.7 mph (6 kph), up to 10 mph (16 kph) in some rapids.

It is unusually steep for a big river, dropping an average of 1.75 feet per mile as it flows through the Canyon.

Mather Point is a good place for the South Rim visitor to consider the North Rim for a moment or two. Over 1,180 feet (360 meters) higher than the South Rim, the thick forests of the Kaibab Plateau are hidden from view. But it can be seen that the slope up from the river is more gradual on the north side and that the edge of the North Rim is much more ragged, more sharply indented by stream valleys, than the South Rim. Both the dense forests and the more severe erosion are the result of the greater precipitation at that higher elevation. When the 16 ½ feet (five meters) of winter snow melts off in spring the streams become powerful tools to cut deep gorges.

Across the Colorado between the high flat lands of the Walhalla Plateau to the east and the Kaibab Plateau to the west is the deep drainage canyon formed by Bright Angel Creek. On the Rim, just to the left of the head of Bright Angel Canyon, is the Grand Canyon Lodge. Its design is adapted so well to the location and blends so well into the North Rim escarpment that, even with binoculars, it is difficult to spot.

At the low end of Bright Angel Canyon is the Kaibab suspension bridge, completed in 1928. It is 440 feet (134 meters) long and 59 feet (18 meters) above the average water level in the river.

It is the link that permits cross-Canyon travel by way of the Bright Angel and South Kaibab Trails on this side of the Colorado and the North Kaibab Trail that follows Bright Angel Creek up the other side of the Canyon.

About 2,625 feet (800 meters) downstream from the Kaibab Bridge a second suspension span was built in 1966, primarily to carry the pipeline that brings water from Roaring Springs on the north slope some 18 ½ miles (30 km) to the waterless South Rim.

It is used by hikers, but mules will not cross it because the river can be seen between the planks. Construction of the North Kaibab Trail was the four-year work of David Rust in the early 1900s. After he finished he planted cottonwoods and fruit trees not far from the river at the lower end of the trail and established Rust Camp as a destination for visitors to the Canyon from the north.

The name was changed to Roosevelt Camp in 1913 after a visit by the President.

It was changed again in 1922 after being remodelled and enlarged according to plans made by the architect of several other Grand Canyon buildings, Mary Jane Colter.

She gave it the name it has held ever since, Phantom Ranch.

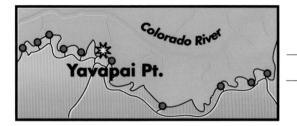

YAVAPAI POINT

(Elevation: 7,090 feet - 2,161 meters)

An alternative name for Yavapai Point is Grandeur Point, a most appropriate name considering the truly wide-angle vistas it affords. Well over half of the Grand Canyon, from Desert View in the east to Havasupai Point in the west, can be seen from here. The view westward from Yavapai Point provides several glimpses of the Bright Angel Trail winding downward from the Rim (elevation: over 6,600 feet, 2,000-plus meters) 4 ½ miles (7.2 km) to Indian Gardens (elevation: over 4,000 feet, 1,200-plus meters) and on another 3 miles (5 km) to the Colorado River at the bridge across to the north side

(elevation: 2,500 feet, 760 meters). It is believed that the trail was originally a bighorn sheep trail that was then used by prehistoric Americans to reach their crop lands on the relatively level bench about ½ mile (almost a kilometer) lower than the Rim. It was surely used by the Hualapai and the Havasupai within historic times.

The trail was widened in 1891 by Pete Berry, who was the proprietor of the Grandview complex, and Ralph and Niles Cameron. Ralph Cameron established control of "Cameron's Trail", as he called it, by filing mining claims along the route. He then set up a toll booth at the trailhead and charged $1.00 for each horse or mule rider to use the trail. His control of the route was disputed by the Santa Fe Company and later by the National Park Service, but to no avail.

He finally gave his rights to Coconino County, but continued to manage the trail and pocketed most of the profits. The South Kaibab and Hermit Trails were built to circumvent Cameron's monopoly on inner-Canyon access. In 1928 Coconino County surrendered jurisdiction of the trail to the Park Service in exchange for construction of a Canyon access road from Williams. At that time the Park Service relocated sections of the trail to improve safety and reduce environmental impact. It also built a caretaker's cabin at Indian Gardens and installed four trailside rest houses. From Yavapai Point the Plateau Point Trail, a 1 ½ mile (2.4 km) spur trail from Indian Gardens out to the edge of the Tonto Platform, is readily visible. The precipitous 1,310-foot (400-meter) drop-off to the river is well worth the trip.

GRAND CANYON VILLAGE

A thousand years ago Native Americans were building on the South Rim of the Grand Canyon. They were hunters and just starting into agriculture. A hundred years ago European Americans began to build here. They were miners and just starting into tourism. John Hance was the first. In 1883 he built a cabin near Grandview Point. Then he built a hotel and established a passenger stage service from Flagstaff. From then on the nature of human enterprise in the area was set in its present mode of visitor service. To work in Grand Canyon is to serve visitors. Even the National Park Service is here to make the area

available to visitors, to preserve the area for the enjoyment of visitors, and to protect the land and the visitors from each other.

J. Wilbur Thurber operated the stage company that provided the link between Flagstaff and Grand Canyon. In 1896, in competition with John Hance and his Grandview Hotel, he built a cabin and set up a few tents near the head of the Bright Angel Trail. His Bright Angel Hotel was at the site of the present Bright Angel Lodge.

The stage ride to the Canyon was long and tiring and expensive – it took 11 uncomfortable hours

and cost $20 – a transportation system begging for improvement. In September of 1901 that improvement arrived. The first trainload of tourists reached the Canyon after only 3 pleasant hours of travel for only $3.95. Because the end of the rail line was some 12 miles (19 km) west of Grandview, the center of activity shifted as a matter of convenience. Grand Canyon Village began to materialize where the railroad up from the south and the Bright Angel Trail up from the river met at the South Rim.

Soon after opening the line to the Canyon the Santa Fe Railway Company set out to improve tourist accommodations on the South Rim. In 1905, when the El Tovar Hotel was completed, those improvements reached a level that can only be described as luxurious. A typical visitor to the Canyon would be someone making a side trip from a transcontinental journey. He would arrive at Grand Canyon by sleeping car and would be transported by surrey to the El Tovar where service and accommodations matched those offered anywhere in the country. Among the services available were tours along the Rim and down the Bright Angel Trail to Indian Gardens or on down to the Colorado River or even up

to the North Rim, crossing the river by means of the swinging bridge, sort of an aerial ferry, that preceded the present suspension bridge. The visitors of early in the century did much the same things that today's visitors do, except they were transported by train and horse-drawn vehicles instead of by busses and cars. Within the Canyon, however, they used mules just as they do now.

The El Tovar is still providing accommodations on the edge of the Canyon and so is the Bright Angel Lodge that replaced Thurber's original collection of tents and cabins. In addition, lodging is now provided at four other sites in the Village: Kachina Lodge, Maswik Lodge, Thunderbird Lodge, and Yavapai Lodge. Overnight dormitory and cabin space is also available at Phantom Ranch. Food service can be obtained at any of the lodging sites and also at the delicatessen in Babbitt's General Store.

As could be expected, the needs and expectations of today's four million visitors a year, arriving at the Canyon by car, bus, plane, or motorhome, are different from those of a few hundred a year travelling by stage or a few thousand a year by train. So Grand Canyon Village, while retaining its historic function of providing destination services for tourists, has both grown and changed over the years. It now includes a bank, a post office, a pharmacy, a medical clinic, a chapel, automobile service and repair facilities, and even a community center and theater.

But many of the old structures also are still part of the Village. Because most of them have been designated

historic structures, they will continue to be preserved and maintained as closely as possible to their original state. For history buffs a tour of these buildings is, of itself, worth a trip to Grand Canyon. The following is a brief description of some of the fascinating old buildings of the historic district:

Red Horse Station – The westernmost of the Bright Angel Lodge cabins is a building of rough-hewn, squared logs which is said to have been built originally at Red Horse Station, one of the three stops on the old stage route at which tired horses were changed for fresh ones and cramped passengers were allowed to relax briefly. The cabin was moved to its present site by Ralph Cameron who added a porch and a second story to make the Cameron Hotel. From 1910 to 1935 the hotel building was the US Post Office. It was then restored to consist of just the original log cabin and became part of the present lodge complex.

Kolb Studio – In 1904 Ellsworth and Emery Kolb built a small photography shop on the rim near the head of Bright Angel Trail. It was enlarged over the years and at one time served also as a dance hall, a movie house, and a soda fountain. Emery Kolb operated his photo and curio shop until his death in 1976, at which time the building reverted to the Park Service.

Lookout Studio – In 1914 Mary Jane Colter designed for the Fred Harvey Company another studio to be built on the rim. She followed the guidelines she had developed from her familiarity with ancient Hopi ruins and produced a low building of rough-cut limestone with an irregular roof line that blends unobtrusively into the rocky cliff.

Buckey O'Neill Cabin – This log cabin is the oldest building on the South Rim and may be the first to have been built here. Early in the 1880s Buckey O'Neill shared ownership in a copper mine 15 miles (24 km) south of the head of the Bright Angel Trail. Despite the distance from his mine, he liked this remote, lonely place enough to build a cabin here. Other than his cabin, which became part of Thurber's Bright Angel Hotel for a time and then was incorporated into Colter's plan for the Bright Angel Lodge, O'Neill's contribution to Grand Canyon Village was the railroad that sparked its development. He had persuaded a mining company to build a rail line to the Canyon to haul ore. When the mining company went bankrupt, the Santa Fe Company bought the half-finished line and completed it to the rim.

Hopi House – Completed in 1905, Hopi House was built to serve as living quarters and workshops for

Hopi craftsmen whose products would be sold along with other souvenirs by the Harvey Company. It, too, was designed by Mary Jane Colter who modelled it after structures in an existing Hopi village named Old Oraibi.

Verkamp's Curios – John G. Verkamp in 1898 rented one of the tents of the Bright Angel Hotel complex and began to sell the sort of curios and crafts that before had been available only in Flagstaff. Business in his tent was slow and he gave up after a couple of weeks. But he still believed the idea was valid. So, in 1905 he returned to the canyon and built Verkamp's Curios at its present location. It is still operated by the Verkamp family.

Santa Fe Railway Station – In 1909, eight years after train service to the Canyon began, the Santa Fe Company built the present station. Its rustic character was a deliberate change from the usual Santa Fe railway stations in order to make it more compatible with the ponderosa forest which surrounds it. The number of visitors arriving at the Canyon by train increased each year until World War II. It then dwindled gradually as both roads and automobiles improved and, in 1968, passenger service was discontinued. It has since been resumed and the station has returned to its proper function.

First NPS Administration Building – The stone and timber structure just east of the railway station and south of Verkamp's Curios was designed by Daniel Hull in the style that became known as "NPS Rustic". It served for many years as the Grand Canyon National Park Administration Building. Later, its interior was modified and it became the residence of the Park Superintendent.

Several other structures in the community that is Grand Canyon Village have been designated historic buildings. Often they can be recognized by the rustic construction of wood and stone that was once thought most appropriate to the setting. Most of them, while retaining their original appearance, have been used for many different purposes. But the *Mule and Horse Barns* have had the same function since they were completed in 1907. Mule rides into the Canyon have always been a favorite activity of visitors and each morning the wranglers and trail guides still assemble at the barns to select and saddle mules that are then led out to the corral at the trailhead to transport people into the Canyon.

Another activity that in recent years has become popular among the more intrepid of Grand Canyon visitors can only be *arranged for* at the Village. Actual running of the Colorado River is begun from an access point upstream of the Canyon, usually Lees Ferry.

Riding a boat through the Grand Canyon is different today from the experience of Major Powell, not only because the boats are different, but also because better techniques have been developed over the

years. Probably the most helpful new technique is not really very new. It was invented by Nathaniel T. Galloway, who used it during the fourth run of the river in 1897. The "Galloway technique" is to navigate the river, especially the rapids, stern first. That allows the oarsman to face in the direction the boat is going, a big help in "reading the river", to slow his movement by normal rowing, and to control his boat better. It has been used by everyone but kayakers ever since. River running, both by individuals in small boats and by guided groups in huge inflated neoprene rafts, has become so popular and, regrettably, so potentially destructive of the inner Canyon that the National Park Service now regulates the activity very strictly. Motorized craft are not allowed, numbers of trips are restricted, and vandalizing of the shoreline and the leaving of trash on the riverbank is prohibited. Open fires also are not permitted because too much of the riparian vegetation was being consumed as fuel. Despite the limitations on river travel necessitated by its popularity, surrendering yourself to the whims of a stream of water rushing through a deep gorge is one of the world's most exhilarating experiences. Modern equipment and experienced boatmen make it much less daring than the 1869 run by John Wesley Powell and his companions – but only slightly less thrilling.

POWELL MEMORIAL

(Elevation: 7,040 feet - 2,145 meters)

Major John Wesley Powell is the man who provided the first real information about the shape and dimensions of the Grand Canyon and about the nature of its geology and life forms.

It is fitting that a monument to his memory has been erected on the South Rim so that visitors gazing in awe at the spectacle can also be reminded of the brave men who first investigated this bizarre terrain in detail.

Powell and nine companions, in 1869, drifted down the waterways from far north at Green River, Wyoming, well past this point to the mouth of the Virgin River in western Arizona.

The purpose of the expedition was to fill in a blank space on the maps of western America.

In 1871 he made a second trip to replace data that was in notes and charts that were lost during the hazardous events of the first trip. He combined his records of both expeditions with the notes and observations of his companions into a book which contains the following lines to tell of the feeling of the explorers at the completion of the trip:

"The relief from danger and the joy of success are great ... Ever before us has been an unknown danger, heavier than immediate peril.

Every waking hour spent in the Grand Canyon has been one of toil. We have watched with deep solicitude the steady disappearance of our scant supply of rations, and from time to time have seen the river snatch of the little left, while we a-hungered ... Now the danger is over, now the toil has ceased, now the gloom has disappeared, now the firmament is bounded only by the horizon ... our joy is almost ecstasy.

We sit till long after midnight talking of the Grand Canyon, talking of home ...".

MARICOPA POINT

(Elevation: 7,000 feet - 2,133 meters)

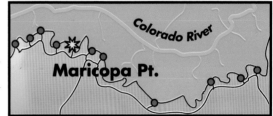

Maricopa Point is the western end of 2.7 paved miles (4.3 kilometers) of the Rim Trail that extends from Mather Point to Hermit's Rest. The eastern end of the paved section is at Yavapai Point.

There is also a paved access from the Village Loop Drive near the Visitor Center and Mather Amphitheater.

Maricopa Point provides a good view of Bright Angle Canyon on the other side of the river. It is a major side canyon that separates two sections of the Colorado Plateau, the Kaibab Plateau and the Walhalla Plateau.

It is actually a minor fault line caused by expansion of the earth's crust that caused it to crack and one side to sink a few feet lower than the other.

Bright Angel Creek follows the fault and has been eroding its way northward into the rim to lengthen and widen its valley.

In another million years or so it may well pinch off the Walhalla Plateau entirely and leave it an island rather than the peninsula it is today.

The side stream and its valley were both named by Major Powell who wrote:

"The little affluent which we have discovered here is a clear, beautiful creek ... We have named one stream, away above, in honor of the great chief of the 'Bad Angels', and as this is a beautiful contrast to that, we conclude to name it 'Bright Angel'."

Between Maricopa Point and the Indian Gardens plateau is a large formation of red rock that has been named The Battleship.

On the Rim to the left is the Orphan Mine, claimed for copper by Daniel Hogan in 1893.

The ore was exceptionally pure but transporting it from this remote area made the operation economically infeasible and mining was soon discontinued.

It was begun again in 1954 when uranium was discovered, and stopped again in 1966. Ownership of the mine reverted to Grand Canyon National Park in 1976.

This Canyon overlook also permits a view, deep in the gorge along the river, of the dark Vishnu Schist with its pink intrusions of granitic gneiss.

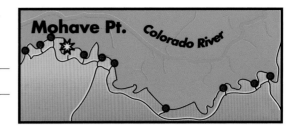

MOHAVE POINT

(Elevation: 6,974 feet - 2,125 meters)

Mohave Point is another good place to appreciate the dangers faced by Powell and his crew. On a quiet day the sound of the torrents of water pounding against the rocks of Hermit Rapids reaches clearly to the Rim. Three sets of rapids can be seen from this point, Hermit, Granite, and Salt Creek. All the major rapids along the Colorado within the Canyon are at the mouths of the tributary streams that brought down from the rims the boulders that cause the rapids. When a severe storm causes flood conditions in the small streams they can wash down additional tons of rocks and the rapids will be changed. Changed, but not moved, because the stream that feeds them rocks will still flow down the same small side canyon. Before the completion of the Glen Canyon Dam in 1963, the Colorado moved a million tons of silt, sand, pebbles, and rocks through Grand Canyon every day. Only about 80,000 tons a day now passes through the Canyon because most of that debris is settling

to the bottom in the quiet waters of Lake Powell. As a consequence, the Glen Canyon Dam and Lake Powell have a maximum estimated life expectancy of only 200 years. Just over a mile (1.8 km) farther along the Rim Drive is *The Abyss*. Here the Great Mohave Wall drops 3,000 feet (900 meters) to the head of Monument Creek on the Tonto Plateau. The difference between the sheer faces of Grand Canyon cliffs such as the Great Mohave Wall and the gentle slopes of platforms such as the Tonto Plateau is entirely the result of differences between the rocks that form them. The cliffs are limestone and sandstone, more resistant to erosion than the shales that form the slopes. When erosion of the shale below them undermines the cliffs they drop away in slices that leave the cliff faces vertical. The Great Mohave Wall was created as a result of erosion of the Bright Angel Shale which makes up the Tonto Plateau. The huge boulders that break away from the cliffs are often carried down to the river to form rapids.

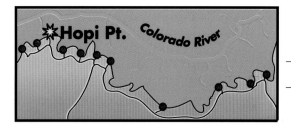

HOPI POINT

(Elevation: 7,071 feet - 2,155 meters)

Almost due north across the Canyon the large, flat-topped butte about 656 feet (200 meters) higher than Hopi Point is Shiva Temple, a section of the Kaibab Plateau that erosion has cut off from the rest of the North Rim and left isolated for thousands of years. Scientists had wondered for years about the possibility that, because of its isolation, Shiva Temple might support life forms that were different from those of the Rims. Such thinking was stimulated by the example of the two tassel-eared squirrel populations that had developed differently on the North and South Rims once they had been isolated from each other by the Canyon.

Despite speculation, there had been no exploration of Shiva Temple until 1937.

That year an American Museum of Natural History expedition, led by Harold E. Anthony, climbed the rock walls of Shiva to study the life of this large "island". News media gave the trip considerable publicity as a "search for dinosaurs".

The results were both disappointing and reassuring. The investigators found no differences between the life forms on Shiva and those on the North Rim. This indicated that either the separation of Shiva from the rest of the Kaibab did not occur all that long ago or that the relatively shallow side canyons between Shiva and the Kaibab did not constitute a serious barrier to North Rim species.

A non-scientific footnote to the expedition report is both puzzling and amusing. A surprising discovery on this long-isolated section of the Canyon was a cardboard box labelled "Eastman Kodak".

Hopi Point provides a good view to the west of a long section of the Colorado, including Granite Rapids at the mouth of Monument Creek. The drainage on the west side of the point is Salt Creek. Horn Creek drains the east side between Hopi Point and the Powell Memorial.

PIMA POINT

(Elevation: 6,720 feet - 2,048 meters)

On the Tonto Plateau, as seen from the western side of Pima Point, outlines of building foundations are faintly visible. They are the remaining signs of what was Hermit Camp, a group of tourist cabins, outbuildings, mule corrals, and a dining hall. It was built in 1911 by the Santa Fe Railway Company as a place in which tourists could spend a quiet night deep within the Canyon itself.

People reached this idyllic spot by riding mules down the tortuous switchbacks of the then newly constructed Hermit Trail, visible from Pima Point and still in use today. Supplies for the most part, however, were lowered to the camp by way of an aerial tramway with cables stretching all the way from the Rim, almost 3,000 feet (900 meters) above.

Hermit Camp was described by an early visitor as providing "accommodations to meet the most fastidious demands ... both for eating and sleeping. Those who wish to sleep in tents or out of doors also will be accommodated." The site is certainly dramatic enough to please. Hermit Creek traces its narrow path through the desert and beyond it is the Lookout, a massive formation whose cap of Redwall Limestone blazes in the setting sunlight. Just across the river is the monolithic Tower of Ra and Pima Point towers in the east.

Hermit Camp was closed in 1930 and the buildings removed, but, in the semi-arid inner canyon, evidence of their former existence will continue to remain for many more years. The site is today a favorite destination for backpacking campers.

Off to the east of Pima Point lies Monument Creek. Over the years it has carried enough boulders down to the Colorado to form the 16-foot (5-meter) ledge of Granite Rapids. Granite and Boucher Rapids farther to the west are two of the more demanding rapids encountered by river runners through the Grand Canyon.

HAVASU FALLS

Framed on the east and west by Grand Canyon National Park is the Havasupai Reservation. It encompasses the land on both sides of Havasu Creek, one of the few permanent streams reaching all the way up to the South Rim. Havasu means "blue-green water" and the Havasupai are the "people of the blue-green water." They and the Hualapai, whose reservation is farther west and entirely on the Rim, are direct descendants of the Cerbat people who moved into this area 150 years after it was abandoned by the Anasazi.

The Havasupai are a small community, only about 300 people. They have always been planters, relying on the mineral-rich water of Havasu Creek to irrigate their gardens. Today they are also, like the European Americans of the South Rim, in the tourist business – but in an intelligently limited way. Their incredibly lovely and idyllic world could easily be severely damaged by an indiscriminate influx of visitors.

So access to Havasu Canyon is not made easy. There is no road within the gorge. There is a trail over which hikers and mule riders travel. There is the Colorado, travelled by river runners. And today there is the air,

through which a few visitors are allowed to travel to the canyon by helicopter. As might be expected there is a waiting list of people seeking an opportunity to visit this Eden.

From the air the upper reaches of Havasu Creek look like a ragged gash in the otherwise level terrain. But, because of the secure and permanent supply of fresh water, the narrow, ribbon-world of Havasu Canyon is a green gash, rich in riparian vegetation and associated wildlife. Waterfowl and hummingbirds are among the bird life and bighorn sheep and beaver are among the mammals. Ringtails, distant relatives of the racoon, are fairly common. But the principal attraction to most visitors is Havasu Creek itself.

A rugged hiking trail parallels the creek as it descends through almost 5,000 feet (1,500 meters) to the Colorado. The trail is steep, but well maintained. And even climbing back up from the river the labor is relieved by the enchanting scenery and the several waterfalls and cascades along the stream. The pools below the falls are favorite spots for bathers. The most popular are those into which Havasu Falls and Mooney Falls drop.

Supplied to a large extent by seepage through the limestone of the Coconino Plateau, the water is a saturated solution of calcium carbonate. As it pours over the edges of rocky shelves slight changes in temperature and pressure cause the dissolved limestone to be precipitated to build terraced ledges of travertine around the pools below.

The life style of the Havasupai appears to be little changed from that of their ancestors. That cultural continuity is partly because of preference, partly because of continued relative isolation, and partly to entertain and encourage tourists. But the people of this small world persist in perpetuating the old ways mostly because those ways constitute a natural adaptation to the environment of Havasu Canyon. If one is going to live in this place, the easiest and best way to do it is the way that has been tried and proven over the centuries. The Havasupai thus continue to be an integrated element of a balanced ecosystem.

NAVAJO BRIDGE

There are three routes from the South Rim of Grand Canyon to the North Rim. You could go on foot or horseback down the Bright Angel Trail or the South Kaibab Trail, cross the Colorado at the suspension bridge at the foot of Bright Angel Creek, and continue up the North Kaibab Trail to the Rim. You could go a mile or so south of Grand Canyon Village to the airport and go over to the North Rim by helicopter. Or, if you wanted to take your car with you, you could go east on the Rim Drive to Desert View, farther east on Arizona Highway 64 to Cameron in the Navajo Reservation, north on US Highway 89 and Alternate US 89 to the Navajo Bridge across the Colorado, west on Alt US 89 to Jacob Lake in the Kaibab National Forest, then south on Arizona 67 to Bright Angel Point on the North Rim. Before 1975 the Navajo Bridge would have had nothing to do with the Grand Canyon except for being part of the highway route from one rim to the other. It crossed the Colorado in Marble Canyon, not Grand Canyon, and it was in Marble Canyon National Monument, not Grand Canyon National Park. Today, Marble Canyon is part of the Park and Navajo Bridge is an important eastern feature.

Marble Canyon was cut by the Colorado River down through the Kaibab Limestone of Marble Platform and into the Toroweap Formation below. Because both these groups of rocks are hard and dense, the banks of Marble Canyon are nearly vertical and the rims are only a little more than the width of the river apart.

The Navajo Bridge is able to cross the Colorado with a single arching structural steel span only 617 feet (188 meters) long. But it supports the roadbed 470 feet (143 meters) above the river.

About 3 miles (5 kilometers) upstream of Navajo Bridge on the north side of the river is Lees Ferry, the put-in point for most Colorado river running.

THE NORTH RIM

The North Rim of the Grand Canyon is part of a geo-political area known as the Arizona Strip, the section of northwestern Arizona that is generally considered bounded by the Nevada border on the west, the Utah border on the north, the Colorado River flowing south through Marble Canyon on the east, and the Grand Canyon on the south. Except for a tiny bit of Interstate 15 in the far northwest corner, there are only two paved roads in this remote area. It is drained of its modest supply of water by the Colorado River and its tributaries.

At 8,200 feet (2,500 meters) above sea level, the North Rim is some 1,214 feet (370 meters) higher than the South Rim. In addition, the shape of the huge Colorado Plateau, the uplands of which both rims are parts, causes the North Rim to slope towards the Canyon, while the South Rim slopes away from it. Those differences, in elevation and direction of drainage, cause other differences that make the North Rim a different world from the Grand Canyon with which most people are familiar.

The greater elevation modifies the climate enough to give the north side of the Canyon more precipitation and cause more of it to be snow. More water has caused faster erosion of the rocks, so the slope of the north wall of the Canyon is gentler than that of the south wall. The Rim is farther back from the river. The streams that drain the North Rim are bigger than most of those on the South Rim, especially in the spring when up to 200 inches (500 cm) of snow melts off. Over the years the larger streams have cut longer and deeper gorges back into the northern edge of the Grand Canyon, dividing it today into four distinct plateau areas that stretch along the 280-mile (450-kilometer) length of the Grand Canyon. Of these separate geographic features the one best known by visitors is the easternmost, the Kaibab Plateau. The Kaibab is also the highest of the four, bounded on both the east and west by the compression foldings of the earth's crust that occurred when it was lifted above the surrounding land 65 million years ago.

The Kaibab Plateau is the only part of the North Rim that is served by paved roads. Access to the Rim is via Arizona Route 67, a 43-mile (70-kilometer) drive south

from the town of Jacob Lake to Bright Angel Point, the center of visitor activities and services. Route 67 is a designated Scenic Route, the Kaibab Plateau North Rim Parkway. At its southern end are Park Service Ranger stations and information centers, automobile service facilities, camp grounds, store, and the Bright Angel Lodge. Several foot trails also begin or end at Bright Angel Point, most notably the North Kaibab Trail down to the Colorado at Phantom Ranch and the suspension bridge that allows access to the South Rim.

North Rim geology almost exactly duplicates that of the South Rim.

The two Rims are capped by the same Kaibab Limestone which was deposited over the same succession of strata. After all, the North and South Rims are the same block of the earth's crust, just sliced into two sections by the Colorado River.

North Rim history is somewhat different, however. The earliest Native Americans were Paiutes who drifted down from farther north while the Anasazi were populating the South Rim. Spanish explorers never quite reached the North Rim of the Canyon. Until the last quarter of the 19th century European American presence in the area was limited to Mormon missionaries. They established river crossings at both ends of the Canyon but learned little of the Canyon itself or its rimlands.

During the 1880s several livestock companies developed in the Arizona Strip and flooded the Kaibab Plateau with range animals. It has been estimated that at one time there were over 100,000 head of cattle and at least 250,000 sheep grazing the then lush grasslands interspersed among the forests. By 1906, when the Grand Canyon National Game Preserve was established, however, most of the ranches had ceased operations. Some blamed the end of ranching on alleged rustling by James Emmett, the operator of Lees Ferry. It is more likely, though, that greedy overgrazing of the fragile land made further ranching unprofitable. When the Game Preserve was established, James T. Owens was made warden. "Uncle Jimmy" for 12 years made a business of mountain lion hunting. His sign read, "Lions Caught to Order, Reasonable Rates". It is believed that he trapped or killed at least 600 lions before changing to bison ranching.

The bison elected to move down off the Rim to the

year-round grazing of the lower House Rock Valley. Owens lived until 1936, sharing summers on the Rim with his half-tame burro, Brighty, and wintering in House Rock Valley with the bison. Brighty, too, would move below the Rim in winter to escape the snow. Today there is a bronze statue of Brighty in the sun room of Grand Canyon Lodge and bison still roam House Rock Valley.

W. W. Wylie developed the first tourist facility on the North Rim in 1917, merely a collection of tents and a cook to prepare meals. In 1923 the Utah Parks Company, a subsidiary of the Union Pacific Railroad, was created and became the designated concessionaire for the North Rim. In 1928 it built an elegant wood and stone lodge on the edge of the Canyon. Designed to blend into the limestone cliff on which it stood, it was barely visible from the South Rim. It was destroyed by fire in 1932, but rebuilt in the same unobtrusive style in 1936, and remains standing today. Rustic log cabins were added to complete the North Rim lodging complex.

After establishing the National Park in 1919 it was only a few years until the North Kaibab Trail was completed through Bright Angel Canyon.

At the lower end of the trail other tourist accommodations were built where the Phantom Ranch is now.

From there it was possible to cross the Colorado by a cable device called a hanging bridge, sort of an aerial ferry, and both hikers and mules were able to reach the South Rim. Rim to Rim travel become much more common, however, after construction of the present suspension bridge in 1928.

Different as the North Rim is from the South Rim, once over the edge into the Canyon itself the two sides of the river become almost indistinguishable.

Although less precipitous as a whole than the south side, the north side still has vertical cliffs of limestone and sandstone and the same panorama of fanciful rock formations that tell the observer that he can be nowhere except in the Grand Canyon of the Colorado River.

BRIGHT ANGEL POINT

(Elevation: 8,145 feet - 2,482 meters)

Bright Angel Point is a long spur extending to the southeast from the Kaibab Plateau between two tributaries of Bright Angel Creek, Roaring Springs and The Transept. As you walk out to the overlook a change in the forest type is noticeable. Because the land near the rim is a bit better drained and because warm currents of air rise up out of the Canyon, conditions on the point are better suited to pinyon pine and juniper trees than to the ponderosa pines that thrive farther back.

Roaring Springs has been the principal source of culinary water for the North Rim for many years. Since a pipe line was completed in 1966, it has provided water for the South Rim as well. The sound of the "roaring" of the springs carries easily to the Rim.

In the middle distance across Bright Angel Creek are three prominent erosional features: from left to right, Deva Temple, Brahma Temple, and Zoraster Temple. On the horizon beyond Deva Temple are the snow-capped peaks of the San Francisco Mountains. The south side of Grand Canyon seems like a vertical wall from this distance.

From Bright Angel Point there is an exceptional view of the unusually long, straight, and deep Bright Angel Canyon. All of those characteristics are because Bright Angel Creek flows along the Bright Angel Fault, a place where the earth's crust was cracked by expansion. Like the Colorado River itself, the creek has cut all the way down to the two-billion-year-old Precambrian rocks. As you follow its impressive canyon off to the right the gently sloping shale of the Tonto Platform can easily be seen resting on the vertical cliff of Tapeats Sandstone. It, in turn, rests on the dark mass of Vishnu Schist to form Major Powell's "Great Unconformity", the gap of 500 million years of geologic history.

A continuation of the course of Bright Angel Canyon leads to Phantom Ranch. Across the river is an indentation in the South Rim where Garden Creek drains Indian Gardens. The buildings of Grand Canyon Village can be seen on the Rim just above it.

THE NORTH RIM FOREST

At its highest elevations the forest of the North Rim is much like the boreal forest of Canada. The principal trees are spruce, fir, and aspen. There are numerous meadows, densely carpeted with grasses and herbs but free of any trees. This vegetative cover and the ecosystem it supports is a remnant of earlier times when the great glaciers farther north made the climate here both colder and wetter. It continues to exist at this latitude only because parts of the Kaibab Plateau are high enough to produce the cold and over 10 feet (the three to four meters) of snow each year it needs for survival.

At lower elevations, but still on the Rim, the dominant tree is the ponderosa pine. Near the edge of the Rim, where more complete drainage leaves a drier soil and there are warm updrafts from the Canyon, the forest changes to pinyon pines and junipers with an occasional Gambel oak.

Each of the forest types has its own distinctive understory of shrubs and herbs. And each has its own community of animals. Among the animals of the North Rim forests is the unique Kaibab squirrel, which lives only among the ponderosa pines of the Kaibab Plateau.

The mule dear is a browser, not a grazer and prefers herbs and shrubs to the once luxurious grasses of these sub-alpine meadows.

After overgrazing destroyed the grass and it was replaced by vegetation more appetizing to the deer, they became common throughout the Rim. Then another human intervention, the elimination of predators, allowed the deer population to overbrowse the region as the domestic herds had overgrazed it. Huge numbers died of starvation before people learned that lions and wolves and eagles and coyotes and bobcats are essential to the balance of this ecosystem. All predators except the wolf have now returned and their populations, as well as that of the deer, are again stable.

The meadows, in which coyotes may be seen hunting mice and voles and on the edges of which wild turkeys may be seen, are caused by drainage sinks in the underlying limestone. After storms and during the spring melt many of the meadows become shallow ponds until the water leaches through the limestone to emerge as springs farther down in the Canyon.

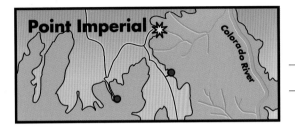

POINT IMPERIAL

(Elevation: 8,803 feet - 2,683 meters)

Point Imperial is the most eastern of the viewpoints along the rims of Grand Canyon. The outlook is toward the east, so it is overlooking a part of the Colorado River that is still following its ancestral course southward along the eastern edge of the Colorado Plateau. The river here has not yet reached the point at which it turns westward to slice through the uplifted land. This is the high side of the East Kaibab Monocline, the fold in the earth's crust that caused the Kaibab Plateau. Point Imperial is almost 3,000 feet (900 meters) higher than the Marble Platform that forms the east bank of the river at this point.

Although the Colorado itself can not be seen from this viewpoint, its very steep eastern wall, known as the Desert Facade, is visible. The successive sedimentary layers can be seen clearly. The top stratum is the Kaibab Limestone that is the surface rock throughout the area. Below that in order are the Toroweap Formation, Coconino Sandstone, Hermit Shale, and the Supai Group. Out of sight below

that the Colorado is flowing in a bed of Redwall Limestone.

Far to the left is a glimpse of Marble Canyon in the vicinity of Lees Ferry. Off to the right the canyon of the Little Colorado can be seen cutting through the Painted Desert of the Navajo Reservation. In the foreground a bit farther to the right is Mt. Hayden, a pinnacle of white Coconino Sandstone resting on red Hermit Shale.

Because of the elevation and the eastern exposure, the forest at Point Imperial is the transition forest in which Engleman spruce, white fir, Douglas fir, and ponderosa pine are all comfortably present. It also grows all the way to the edge of the Rim without the usual transition to pinyon-juniper forest. This ponderosa pine-fir mix supports a variety of birds and mammals that includes two kinds of jay, several woodpeckers, three different chipmunks, two tree squirrels and one porcupine, but is too cold for most reptiles.

WALHALLA PLATEAU

(Elevation: 7,994 feet - 2,436 meters)

The Walhalla Plateau is a peninsula of the Kaibab Plateau extending southward toward the Colorado. It is 23 miles (37 kilometers) from the Bright Angel Lodge along one of the most scenic roadways in the National Park. The Walhalla Plateau itself is 15 miles (24 kilometers) long, covered by a mature forest of ponderosa pine. Cape Royal is at its southern tip, five miles (eight kilometers) from the river. At the base of the peninsula where it joins the main body of the Kaibab Plateau the Walhalla is quite narrow, just over a

mile (only a couple of kilometers) wide.

It is jokingly said that if you want to drive out to the Walhalla Plateau, you should plan to do so within the next million years because after that time headward erosion of Bright Angel Creek will have made it an unreachable island. Until then, however, it is a pleasant drive through the forest and a respite from the vast splendor of most of Grand Canyon.

The ponderosa pine forest is the only habitat of the Kaibab squirrel, so along the road to Cape Royal is a fine place to see this unique animal. Its bushy white tail is easy to spot as it scurries about, pausing to nibble its dietary staple, the tiny seeds of the ponderosa.

Undergrowth is limited in the pine forest and the ground is carpeted with pine needles, over a foot deep in spots. A mature forest such as this is unlikely to regenerate itself unless small catastrophes open spaces into which the sun can reach young seedlings. So fire, once thought to be the enemy of the forest, is actually essential. But, like any medicine, it is good only in measured doses.

Too much is deadly. So the usually small fires caused by lightning strikes during a storm are welcome therapy to the forest. They burn off the layer of needles and small dead branches and the undergrowth without damaging the trees that are insulated by their thick bark.

The result is a sunny, nutrient-rich forest in which young seedlings may sprout and thrive.

ANASAZI RUINS

The prehistoric peoples who have lived in and near the Grand Canyon have been mentioned several times in this guide to the area. Many of the place names in Grand Canyon National Park are reminders of them and of the continuing presence of their descendants. The following is a brief summary of what the archeologists have deduced, or have surmised about those early peoples.

First there were the Split Twig People who, about 2,000 BC, bent and entwined split willow twigs to form representations of animals. They left these figures in limestone caves in the Canyon walls. Because there are so few other signs of these people and because some of the animal figures are pierced, spear-like, by other twigs, it is believed that they were prayerful offerings to bring success to primitive hunters. During the following centuries either those people, or others who had moved into the region, exhibited greater advancement and left more evidence of their presence. These later people built pithouses for shelter and made baskets. So little else is known about them that the archeologists have been forced to call them simply the "Basketmakers."

The next occupants of the area are thought to have moved in about 600 or 700 AD. They have been called Anasazi, a Navajo word meaning "ancient ones", but the archeologists usually refer to them as the Pueblo People because they lived in small village-like communities. The Pueblos still hunted and gathered wild foods – they had invented both the spear thrower and the bow and arrow – but they also cultivated plants and made pottery for safe storage of their crops.

Among the open spaces within the ponderosa pine forest of the Walhalla Plateau are some that contain signs of these Anasazi. More than 100 "farm" sites have been identified. At each of these garden plots where corn, beans, and squash were cultivated there is usually the remains of a small, one-room structure that archeologists have called "field houses". These were perhaps homes for a single "farmer" and his family.

Walhalla Glades is a much larger site, consisting of at least nine rooms and perhaps serving as storehouses and quarters for twenty or more persons. Here are the remains of rock walls constructed at least 900 years ago.

When this site was excavated the walled areas were found to be filled with enough rock rubble to indicate that the standing blocks were not just foundations, but that the entire walls had been made of shaped limestone blocks mortared together with adobe. Within the stubs of the walls they also found fragments of wooden beams and more adobe, materials such as would have been used to make a roof. Since there is no evidence of doorways, it is assumed that entry was made through holes in the roof that were reached by ladders placed against the walls. It is thought that the Pueblos occupied the Walhalla Plateau only during the summers. When cold weather put an end to the growing season the people would take their stored harvest down into the warmth of the Canyon, possibly to the large pueblo on the Unkar delta. There is indication that earlier the population of the Unkar settlement had gradually grown until the available farm land there was no longer sufficient to support it. It was then that summer cultivation began on the Rims and Walhalla Glades is a result.

For some 600 years the Anasazi, the Ancient Ones, the Pueblos, lived and farmed in and about the Grand Canyon. Remains of at least 2,500 building sites have so far been discovered. These sites range from single small constructs to protect something or someone from predators or the weather to complex structures like the Unkar ruins or Walhalla Glades. And then, about 1250 AD, they left, perhaps forced by a succession of dry years to find a more reliable source of water.

According to archeologists, today they are called Hopis and they live in central New Mexico.

Cape Royal

CAPE ROYAL

(Elevation: 7,865 feet - 2,398 meters)

At the end of the drive through the forest is Cape Royal, a promontory that projects well out into the Canyon and provides a panoramic view in excess of 180 degrees. From the parking area and picnic ground a self guiding nature trail about half a mile (less than a kilometer) long leads to observation points on the Rim. As you walk this trail it is immediately noticeable that the vegetation has changed. The ponderosas have given way to the "pigmy forest" of pinyon pines and junipers. Again, this is the effect of more thorough drainage close to the edge of the Canyon and warm currents of air rising from the desert-like regions below. This particular pinyon-juniper forest is also mature and well developed with an abundant understory of mountain mahogany, serviceberry, blackbrush, cliffrose, and buffaloberry. Limited amounts of sagebrush are also present, as are pricklypear cactus and yuccas.
The view from the eastern Canyon overlook shows the meander in the Colorado where Unkar Creek

has washed boulders to create Unkar Rapids. The gravelly delta at the mouth of the creek is the site of one of the latest of the many Anasazi settlements within the Grand Canyon area, believed to have been abandoned about 1125 AD. Raising your line of sight straight up from that glimpse of the river reveals the watch tower at Desert View.
In the foreground almost due south is the prominent formation named Vishnu Temple and just up from that are the San Francisco Mountains.
The view to the west from Cape Royal is of the most familiar part of Grand Canyon. Many of the overlooks and features of the South Rim can be seen from here. Many of the erosional features on the north side of the Colorado are also visible. The three temples that were prominently visible from Bright Angel Point, Deva, Brahma, and Zoroaster, are here seen from their other sides. The Tonto Platform (Tonto Plateau) is prominent and the difference in slope of the two sides of the Canyon is apparent.

TOROWEAP OVERLOOK

(Elevation: 4,520 feet - 1,377 meters)

In the western part of the North Rim, accessible by 66 miles (107 kilometers) of dirt road from Fredonia, Arizona, is Toroweap Point. It is considerably lower than most of the North Rim partly because, strictly speaking, it is not the Rim. What is usually thought of as the Rim is here called the "outer rim" and is some 5 miles (8 kilometers) north across a broad platform called the Esplanade. Toroweap is at the top of a steep-walled gorge about half a mile (nearly a kilometer) high that drops almost vertically to the river. Also here on the edge of the Esplanade at the mouth of Toroweap Valley is Vulcan's Throne, a cinder cone ¾ mile (1.2 kilometers) wide and 574 feet (175 meters) high.

An observation point just beyond the western edge of the campground provides one of the Park's most spectacular views of the Canyon. About a million years ago a series of lava flows poured over the edge of the Esplanade from the north and dammed the Colorado with hot rock. This happened not once, but several times. Each time the river was impounded behind the basaltic dam and each time it eventually broke through and cut back to its original level. What is left of that vulcanism are the lava cascades on the north side of the river, a few pockets of lava rock clinging to the south wall, and Lava Falls, the largest and most dangerous rapids in the Canyon.

The volcanic rocks, unusual after so many miles of drifting among sedimentary layers, were noted and investigated by Major John Wesley Powell and his group. Major Powell's journal contains the entry,

"What a conflict of water and fire there must have been here! Just imagine a river of molten rock running down into a river of melted snow. What a seething and boiling of the waters; what clouds of steam rolled into the heavens!"

The south bank of the Colorado and the land of the South Rim at this point is beyond the western edge of Grand Canyon National Park. It is instead part of the Hualapai Reservation and administered by the Hualapai Tribe.

Toroweap

Kanab
Rapids

Colorado River

Deer
Creek
Falls

Tapeats Creek

KAIBAB

Steamboat
Mtn
EL. 7422

Gatagama
Point

Tahute Point
EL. 6508

Great Thumb
Point
EL. 6749

Swamp
Point

GREAT THUMB MESA

Fossil
Canyon

Fossil Bay

POWELL
PLATEAU

GRAND

Muav Canyon

White Creek

Emerald
Point

Shinumo Creek

Shunono Amphi

Holy Grail
Temple

King Arthur
Castle

Mooney Falls

Havasu Falls

Navajo Falls

Supai Falls

SUPAI
EL. 3195

Havasu Springs

Forster Canyon

Wheeler
Point

Marcos
Terrace

Apache
Point

Mount
Huethawali
EL. 6275

GRANITE

Sagittarius Ridge

HUALAPAI TRAIL

CATARACT

SUPAI TRAIL

Topocoba
Hilltop

ARCH

Havasupai
Point

Cataract Creek

HAVASUPAI INDIAN RESERVATION

CANYON

Aztec

Royal Arch Creek

Amphitheater

GORGE

Turquoise Canyon

Slate Creek

SOU

Bou

The altitudes are shown in feet (1 foot = 30.48 cm).

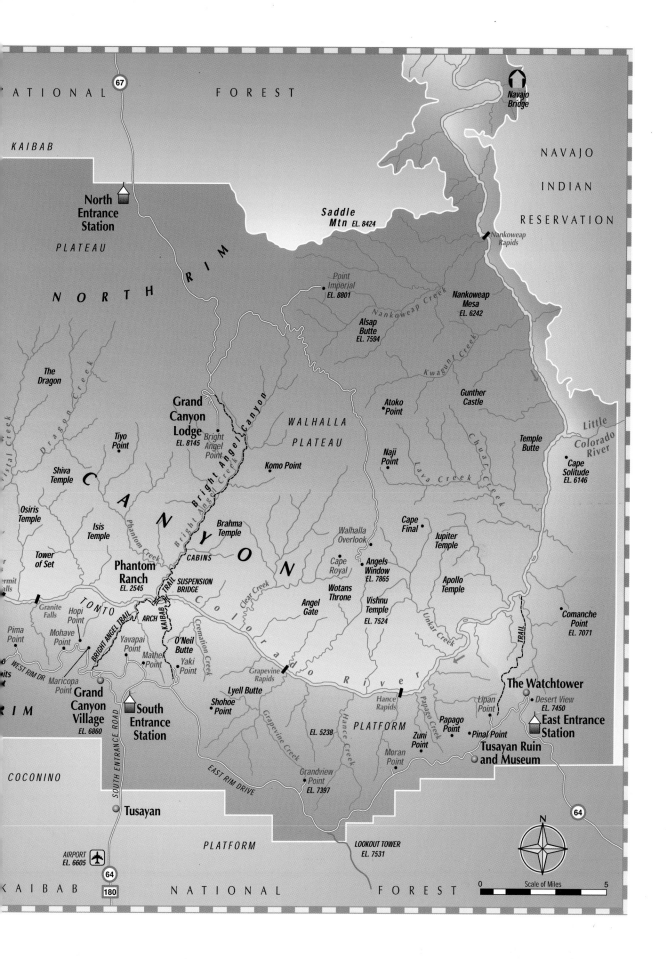

INDEX